FIVE-MINUTE BIBLE FUN, LESSON OPENERS

by Elizabeth Whitney Crisci

illustrated by
Corbin Hillam

Cover by Vanessa Filkins
Shining Star Publications, Copyright © 1991
A Division of Good Apple
ISBN No. 0-86653-571-3
Standardized Subject Code TA ac
Printing No. 9876543

Shining Star Publications
A Division of Good Apple
1204 Buchanan St., Box 299
Carthage, IL 62321-0299

DEDICATION

Dedicated to the teachers at Second Baptist Church of Newton Upper Falls who faithfully give of their time and energy to serve the Lord through the Sunday school and weekday programs.

INTRODUCTION

Five-Minute Bible Fun, Lesson Openers is a compilation of easy-to-use, fun-to-do activities to help students enjoy participating in Bible learning. They are to be used to guide the minds of the children into a learning attitude. They will serve as mind openers to make the lesson easier to learn and more exciting to listen to.

The Lesson Openers are listed in five different categories. Each Lesson Opener should be read in advance of the lesson period so the teacher may be assured of understanding it and have time to prepare if necessary.

Each Lesson Opener is not meant to be a time consumer, but an honest preparation for the subject of the day. These ideas are helpful in making the students arrive on time for class—they will miss something special if they are late!

Use *Five-Minute Bible Fun, Lesson Openers* with prayer and discernment. Make even the beginning of each class count for God and watch how the students love to come to class. What a privilege to share the Bible with eager students! God bless each teacher of the Word.

TABLE OF CONTENTS

Shining Star Publications, Copyright © 1991, A division of Good Apple.
SS895

ARTS AND CRAFTS

Shining Star Publications, Copyright © 1991, A division of Good Apple   SS895

COOKIE DOUGH FUN

Time involved: Four or five minutes

Supplies: Cookie dough from a mix or from baking ingredients, nearby church oven, cookie sheets, hand washing facilities, waxed paper, toothpicks, spatula.

Purpose: To have informal fun with your precious students and to make an important impression on the minds of the students.

How-to for COOKIE DOUGH FUN:

Before class, mix cookie dough that is firm enough to be molded into shapes. Have the children wash and dry their hands. Divide the dough into small handfuls and ask the students to shape their dough into a symbol of the lesson. If the lesson is about the death of Jesus, the cross is an appropriate symbol to form. If the lesson is on feeding the five thousand, the shape of a fish would be appropriate. Allow them a few minutes to work on waxed paper. With a toothpick, let them scratch their initials on their cookies. Have the students place their cookies onto a cookie sheet. Bake. Serve at the end of the class.

NOW, SCRATCH YOUR INITIALS ON.

SS895

YARN WORDS

Time involved: Five minutes

Supplies: Construction paper (4″ × 6″), either have glue in individual bottles with nozzles or pour glue into dishes and use with paint brushes, brightly colored yarn, scissors, pencils.

Purpose: To fix the important word of the lesson in the center of the students' minds, both during class and during the following week.

How-to for YARN WORDS:

When a lesson has a special word that brings it all together, like *pray*, *share*, *sing*, or *forgive*, try YARN WORDS. Give the children construction paper and ask them to write, in cursive, the word of the day. Let them choose a contrasting color of yarn. The students must go over the pencil lines with white glue. They must do it quickly, and then lay the yarn out over the glue and let dry. The word will stay in their minds for a long time.

SS895

DOTS AND DOTS

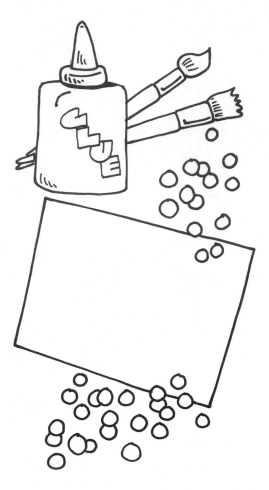

Time involved: Four or five minutes

Supplies: Thinned white glue, paint brushes, construction paper (5½″ × 8″), several hundred prepunched white dots.

Purpose: To enable the students to think about the subject and respond in an interesting way.

How-to for DOTS AND DOTS:
Choose several ideas that would set each child's mind in the right direction. For example, if the lesson is on Moses crossing the Red Sea, pictures could be:
    a river scene
    a man with a staff in his hand
    the word *GO*

If the lesson is about Jesus calming the sea, the picture could be:
    a boat
    big waves
    the word *PEACE*

Give the students about five minutes to glue dots in place for their pictures. If time allows, let children share their pictures with the group at the end of the class.

CHOOSE A PICTURE AND GLUE THE DOTS.

SS895

TWO-CRAYON ART

Time involved: Four minutes

Supplies: Crayons, rubber bands, white paper (approximately 8½" × 11").

Purpose: To teach creativity to the students and to allow them to open their minds to the subject of the lesson.

How-to for TWO-CRAYON ART:
Ask the children to choose their two favorite colors. They must put a rubber band around the crayons in such a way that the points of the crayons meet exactly on one end. Then let them make pictures of their houses, a Bible, a mountain, a fish, a lake, or scenes that will introduce the lesson of the day. Let them write their names in two colors, too, and place the pictures on the bulletin board.

SS895

CUT UPS

Time involved: Five minutes

Supplies: Scissors and construction paper (approximately 4½″ × 9″).

Purpose: To practice eye-hand coordination and focus on the subject of the lesson.

How-to for CUT UPS:
Make samples of CUT UPS and show to the class. Give each child a piece of construction paper and a pair of scissors. After announcing the Bible lesson for the day, students are to cut out a shape that will depict the subject of the lesson. Explain that they cannot use pencils or pens to draw the outline of the shape. They must cut it freehand. If the lesson is on Joshua, a trumpet, a group of people marching, or a long cord hanging out of a window would be appropriate. If the lesson is on Jesus helping the disciples catch fish, the CUT UPS could be the shape of a fish, a boat, a fishing net, or an oar. Allow time for the children to share their CUT UPS.

Cut out a picture.

Shining Star Publications, Copyright © 1991, A division of Good Apple

SS895

OPEN DOORS

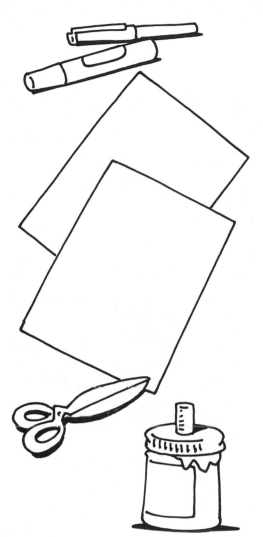

Time involved: Five or six minutes

Supplies: One piece each of construction paper (9″ × 12″) and white typing or copier paper (9″ × 12″) for each student, felt-tip markers, pointed scissors, glue or rubber cement.

Purpose: To arouse curiosity in students and to get them ready for an exciting lesson.

How-to for OPEN DOORS:

Let the students draw two squares on their construction paper. Then, they must cut three sides of their squares and fold up on the fourth side. Place the construction paper on top of the white paper and trace the squares onto the white paper. Remove the construction paper and set aside. Have the students print given words for the coming lesson on the left square on the white paper in fancy print. On the right square they must draw a picture that reveals the meaning of the word. The word might be *pray*, *sing*, *love*, *study*, or *trust*. It should be an impromptu picture, so allow only five minutes for the entire process. Finally, glue the construction paper onto the white paper (one dot of glue or rubber cement in each corner). Have the students set their OPEN DOORS aside until an appropriate place during the lesson when the teacher can use the OPEN DOORS as an illustration to emphasize the lesson.

white paper

construction paper

Shining Star Publications, Copyright © 1991, A division of Good Apple SS895

PLASTER CAST

Time involved: Five minutes

Supplies: A package of plaster of Paris, a plastic (throw away) mixing bowl, a mixing spoon, waxed paper sheet for each student (approximately 8½" × 11"), old newspapers, toothpicks.

Purpose: To allow students to concentrate on a subject and create something to remind them of it.

How-to for PLASTER CAST:

As the students arrive for class, begin mixing the plaster of Paris. Have the sample available, but let the students choose a shape to be used for their own plaster casts. If the lesson is on feeding the five thousand, the cast can be shaped into a fish or loaf of bread, a field, a boy, a basket or whatever the student decides. If the lesson is on the plagues in Egypt, the students can make a lamb, a grasshopper, a brick, or whatever they would like. Give the students a glob of plaster of Paris and let them mold it on their waxed paper, which has been placed on old newspapers to avoid a mess on the table. After several minutes, let the children engrave their initials on their creations with toothpicks. Set it aside until the next week when they can color it with felt markers and then review their lesson.

plaster of Paris

waxed paper

newspaper

MAKE A SHAPE TO GO WITH THE STORY.

UNDER GLASS

Time involved: Five minutes

Supplies: Permanent felt-tip markers, small but simply colored pictures such as greeting cards, clear glass (approximately 4″ × 6″) with well-taped edges, tape.

Purpose: To show the beauty of God's creation.

How-to for UNDER GLASS:
Give each child a piece of glass. Let each child choose a picture and tape it under the glass with the picture showing through. With permanent markers, children are to trace and color the picture. When they are finished drawing and coloring their pictures, carefully remove the picture that was taped to the back of the glass. A beautiful picture will emerge.

MY PICTURE IS OF GOD'S CREATION.

SS895

HOLE FUN

Time involved: Five minutes

Supplies: Computer paper with holes still attached along the sides, pencils.

Purpose: To teach the children creativity while whetting their appetites for learning the lesson of the day.

How-to for HOLE FUN:
Give each child a half sheet of computer paper (cut lengthwise down the middle so that one edge has holes). After the subject for the day's lesson has been given, children are to incorporate the holes into appropriate drawings. If time allows, share drawings at the end of the class meeting.

MAKE THE HOLES
PART OF YOUR
PICTURE.

MANNA FROM HEAVEN

SS895

PRESSED FLOWERS

Time involved: Five minutes

Supplies: Petals from flowers (small petals are best), waxed paper, white glue, lightweight card-board (4" × 6"), pens.

Purpose: To show God's creation and fix a brief Bible verse or theme in the students' minds.

How-to for PRESSED FLOWERS:
Several weeks ahead of time, strip the petals from several flowers. You will need enough for each child to have ten to twenty small petals. Place the flower petals between sheets of waxed paper and put in a book. Place several heavy books on top to press flowers. Leave for several weeks. Before the class is to meet, carefully remove the dried, pressed flower petals from the waxed paper. Children are to glue the pressed flowers to bookmark-sized pieces of cardboard. Add a Bible verse or phrase to each bookmark. Cover with clear Con-Tact paper.

GLUE THE PRESSED FLOWERS TO YOUR BOOKMARK.

ALL THINGS CREATED BY HIM

   SS895

FAN FUN

Time involved: Five minutes

Supplies: Heavyweight white paper (6″ square), felt-tip markers, staple gun, Popsicle sticks.

Purpose: To make a pretty reminder of the lesson to take home and to set the atmosphere for a fun lesson.

How-to for FAN FUN:

First, have each student make a simple picture with felt markers that will introduce a lesson subject. If the lesson is on the Creation, perhaps an animal picture would be appropriate. If the lesson is on Christ's Crucifixion, a picture of the three crosses would be appropriate. Next, let students fold the pictures diagonally, putting opposite corners together. Then, carefully fold each side to look like a fan. Finally, staple the corner to a Popsicle stick.

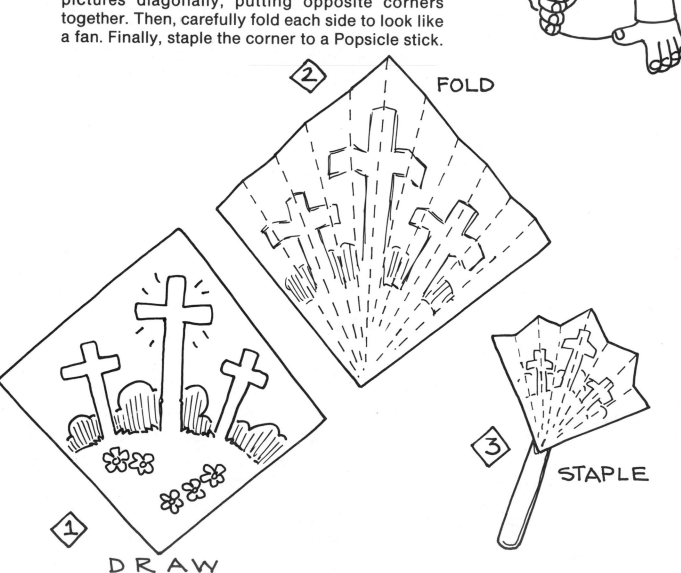

2 FOLD

1 DRAW

3 STAPLE

MAKE YOUR OWN STICKER

Time involved: Four minutes

Supplies: Plain white stickers (like mailing stickers), fine-tip felt markers.

Purpose: To satisfy the children's desire for stickers, to introduce a lesson and to make the opening moments enjoyable.

How-to for MAKE YOUR OWN STICKER:
Decide on a one-word motto or idea that will introduce the lesson. For example, if the lesson is to be on Samuel, the word could be *listen* and the sticker could include an ear. If the lesson is to be on Thomas, the word could be *doubt* and the picture could be a hand or a sad face. Encourage the children to cover the stickers with color to make them look like purchased stickers. They may wear their stickers or put them on their day's work.

SS895

LACE OVERS

Time involved: Five minutes

Supplies: Brightly colored (red, orange, blue) construction paper cut in 4" × 8" pieces, 2"-wide open lace, white glue, black marker.

Purpose: To make an attractive reminder of an important lesson.

How-to for LACE OVERS:
Let children choose colors of construction paper and give them a piece of lace. They are to glue the lace along the bottom of their construction paper and print a one word remembrance for the lesson. For example, if the lesson is on Jesus' childhood, *growth* would be appropriate. If the lesson is on Noah, the word *faith* could be written. Have the students put their names on the back side of the LACE OVERS and hang them on the bulletin board for a week before taking them home.

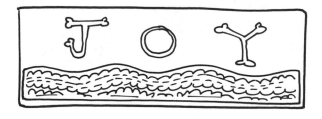

SS895

TILE ART

Time involved: Five minutes

Supplies: Sample tiles from a tile company or left-overs from a home job, permanent markers, rulers, scrap paper, pencils.

Purpose: To let the children express themselves artistically and to put the important idea of the coming lesson into their homes as a remembrance.

How-to for TILE ART:

Give each child a tile, a piece of scrap paper and a pencil. Let the children look at the sample. Ask them to illustrate the given theme of the day: *faith, hope, love, peace,* or *joy*. They should use the word and incorporate it into their TILE ART. When they have a nice drawing on the scrap paper, give them permanent markers and let them transfer their art onto the tile. It can't be erased; encourage them to know what they want to draw on the tile before they begin.

SS895

DIAMOND ART

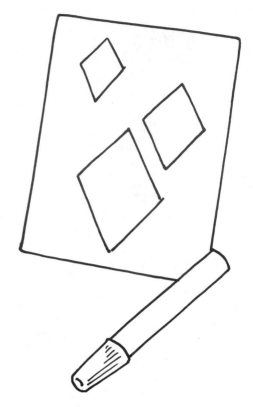

Time involved: Four minutes

Supplies: White paper (8½" × 11"), felt-tip pens or ballpoint pens.

Purpose: To let the children show their creativity, to let them practice following directions, and to introduce the lesson of the day.

How-to for DIAMOND ART:

For a sample, the teacher should draw three diamond shapes (small, medium and large) on a sheet of the white paper. Inside the three diamonds, pictures should be drawn that will make the subject of the upcoming lesson obvious. For example, if the lesson is on Judas' betrayal of Jesus, the small picture might be money, the medium picture might be a sly look on Judas' face, and the large picture might be Judas leading the soldiers. Show the sample and let the children draw what they think will introduce a lesson. Let them do it in markers or pens. For the very young, before class, draw the three diamonds on each paper. (If there is a copier nearby, make one and copy the others.)

DRAW 3 QUICK PICTURES TO TELL THE STORY.

SS895

PLASTIC BAG ART

Time involved: Five minutes

Supplies: Plastic Ziploc sandwich bags (one per child), liquid poster paint.

Purpose: To experiment with a new art form and to fix a theme in each student's mind.

How-to for PLASTIC BAG ART:

Give each child a plastic Ziploc sandwich bag. Into each bag place a tablespoon of brightly colored poster paint. Carefully seal each bag. Use hands to gently spread the paint inside the bag until it is smooth. Using a finger, the child can spell out important words or draw a simple shape to celebrate the theme of the lesson. Children can smooth and rewrite or redraw pictures as many times as they wish. Place the bags on a display table. They can be used again; the paint will not dry out immediately.

SS895

PIN FUN

Time involved: Four or five minutes

Supplies: Large flat pins (approximately 1½" in diameter) or milk bottle caps with pins attached (premade by teacher), white Con-Tact paper, fine-tip permanent markers, scrap paper.

Purpose: To encourage creativity and send home a message about the lesson.

How-to for PIN FUN:

On scrap paper, let the children make a quick design for the given theme of the day. If the lesson is on missions, a small map with the word *GO* would be good. If the lesson is on the Creation, a picture of anything God created could be on the pin with the word *God* printed by it. Give children 1½" circle of white Con-Tact paper and let them sketch their picture on it. Color in with markers. Let them stick their circle to the top of a large flat pin. Let them wear their pins home.

CLOTHESPIN CRAFT

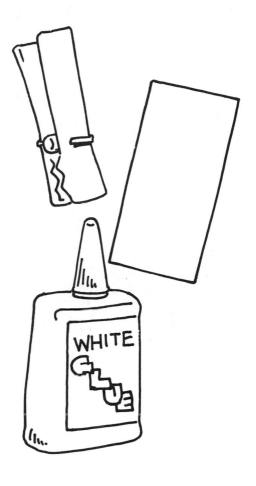

Time involved: Five minutes

Supplies: Clip clothespins, small pieces (2″ × 3″) of lightweight cardboard, white glue, paint brushes, Bible stickers, fine-tip felt markers, scrap paper (cut in 2″ × 2″ squares).

Purpose: To enable the students to make a remembrance of the class for home.

How-to for CLOTHESPIN CRAFT:
Give each student a clip clothespin and a small piece of cardboard. Students may share the felt pens. They should draw a picture to remember the Bible verse of the day. If the verse is "For God so loved the world . . . ," they might draw a world; if the verse is "Let not your heart be troubled . . . ," they might draw a heart; if the verse is "The Lord is my shepherd . . . ," they might draw a sheep. Give them a sticker to place on the cardboard with the Bible verse on it. They can attach the clip clothespin to the cardboard with the white glue. Set aside to dry. Send it home at the end of class. Give them a thought, a homework assignment, a missionary picture, or blank memo paper to place in the clip for home.

SS895

FINGERNAIL DELIGHTS

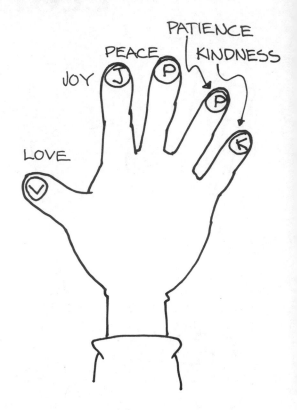

Time involved: Five minutes

Supplies: About one-quarter yard of brightly colored Con-Tact paper, fine-tip felt markers, scissors.

Purpose: To have fun with an intriguing introduction to a Bible lesson.

How-to for FINGERNAIL DELIGHTS:

The teacher can wear sample FINGERNAIL DE-LIGHTS and show them as the class begins. This is a good project when a list is to be learned. The nails will work for remembering the fruits of the Spirit or the epistles of Paul. Give each student a 1" × 6" piece of Con-Tact paper. Have each child draw fingernails on the Con-Tact paper. Then, with markers, let each one print the first letter of each *fruit* or *epistle* on each fingernail in turn. Cut out each nail and place in order on fingers. Then repeat the list once or twice during the class period.

GOLD LEAF SPECIAL

Time involved: Five minutes

Supplies: Plastic covers from juice cans (approximately 2½" in diameter), gold paint, black fine-tip permanent markers, magnet.

Purpose: To encourage creativity and make a magnet to remind students often of the Bible lesson.

How-to for GOLD LEAF SPECIAL:
Give each child a plastic cover and a paint brush and a few minutes to paint the cover gold. (No need to paint the back.) Let it dry. During the lesson the children are to think about a picture or a phrase to draw on the GOLD LEAF SPECIAL. If the class is studying the Beatitudes, the word *Blessed* or a happy face could be printed on it. If the lesson is on the calming of the sea by Jesus, lightning or a rough sea could be drawn, or the word *Peace* could be printed on it. At the end of the class, when the gold paint is dry, let each child draw his own thing! Glue the magnet onto the back of the GOLD LEAF SPECIAL.

CREATIVE WRITING

UNENDING SONG

Time involved: Four or five minutes

Supplies: Chalkboard and chalk.

Purpose: To gather the attention of the children and to make the introduction to the lesson a fun time and a learning experience.

How-to for UNENDING SONG:

Choose a familiar tune like "The Farmer in the Dell" and think of a few words that will fit the theme of the day. For example, if the lesson will be on prayer, the words for the unending song might be:

> I'll talk to God each day,
> I'll talk to God each day,
> Hi, ho, my God is good,
> I'll talk to Him each day.

Or,

> I won't forget to pray . . .
> Let's pray for our mom and dad . . .
> Let's pray for our teacher . . .

Let the children add verses of their own until five minutes have elapsed; then, on to the lesson.

SS895

FINISH ME UP

Time involved: Three or four minutes

Supplies: Small papers (4" × 6"), pencils.

Purpose: To allow the students to have input into an important subject, show them the value of their ideas, and encourage them to change their ideas when they do not coincide with Scripture.

How-to for FINISH ME UP:
Choose a sentence that will help set the minds of the students in the right direction. For example, if the lesson is on obedience, a good beginning sentence would be: "It's hard to obey my parents when . . ." If the lesson is on trusting Jesus, a good beginning sentence might be: "It's hardest to trust Jesus during . . ." If the lesson is on forgiveness, a good sentence beginning might be: "The last time I asked God to forgive me . . ." Allow about three minutes for the children to finish their sentence. Then ask each one to read what he has written. With minds centered in the right direction, begin the lesson!

SS895

MAKE IT

Time involved: Five minutes

Supplies: White construction paper or white typing paper, fine-tip markers.

Purpose: To say thank you to a leader in the church and bring seriousness to the task of working for the Lord.

How-to for MAKE-IT:

Give students a piece of paper and ask them to fold it in half. On the cover they can print *Thank you* in fancy letters. On the inside they can draw a picture and a word of thanks to the pastor, the superintendent or someone they appreciate in the church. Let them hand deliver it to the proper person at the end of class.

Shining Star Publications, Copyright © 1991, A division of Good Apple

SS895

ADD A WORD

Time involved: Five minutes

Supplies: Overhead projector, one transparency, transparency pen, blank wall or screen.

Purpose: To stimulate discussion on a particular subject and encourage children.

How-to for ADD A WORD:

Explain the directions to the children. The teacher will help put one word on the overhead and the students, in order, will have to add one word. The sentence will have to make sense and it must be on the lesson of the day. If the lesson is on parents, the sentence might be: "How to get along with parents." If the lesson is on David and Jonathan's friendship, the sentence might be: "How to choose the right friends." When the sentence is complete and each student has added a word, reread the sentence and immediately plunge into the lesson.

SS895

LAST LETTERS

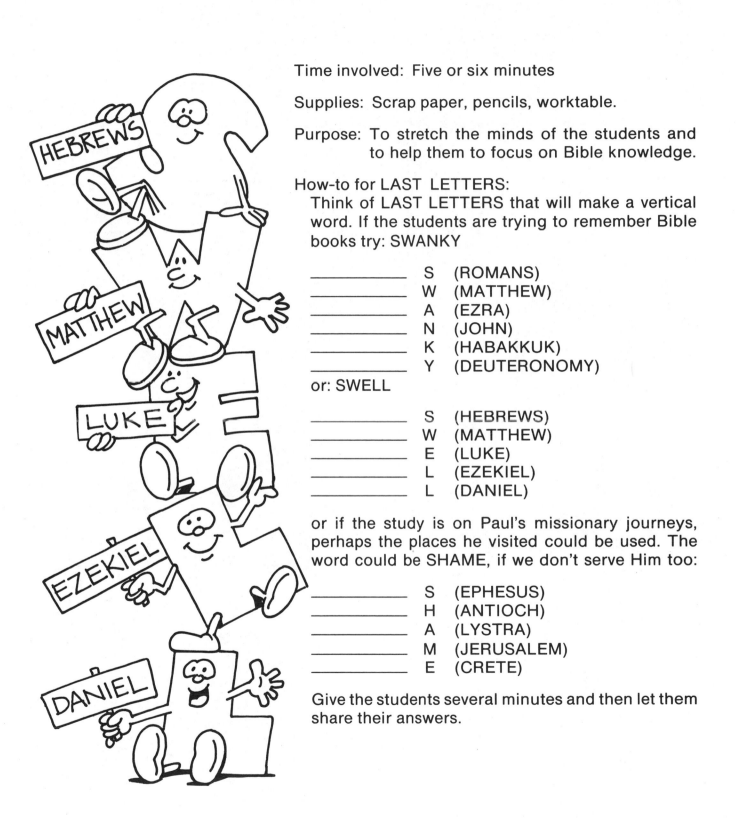

Time involved: Five or six minutes

Supplies: Scrap paper, pencils, worktable.

Purpose: To stretch the minds of the students and to help them to focus on Bible knowledge.

How-to for LAST LETTERS:
Think of LAST LETTERS that will make a vertical word. If the students are trying to remember Bible books try: SWANKY

_____	S	(ROMANS)
_____	W	(MATTHEW)
_____	A	(EZRA)
_____	N	(JOHN)
_____	K	(HABAKKUK)
_____	Y	(DEUTERONOMY)

or: SWELL

_____	S	(HEBREWS)
_____	W	(MATTHEW)
_____	E	(LUKE)
_____	L	(EZEKIEL)
_____	L	(DANIEL)

or if the study is on Paul's missionary journeys, perhaps the places he visited could be used. The word could be SHAME, if we don't serve Him too:

_____	S	(EPHESUS)
_____	H	(ANTIOCH)
_____	A	(LYSTRA)
_____	M	(JERUSALEM)
_____	E	(CRETE)

Give the students several minutes and then let them share their answers.

SS895

BEEHIVE OF FUN

Time involved: Four minutes

Supplies: Chalkboard and chalk (or poster board and wide-tip felt pen), scrap paper, pencils, worktable.

Purpose: To encourage students to think of how they should act as believers in Jesus Christ.

How-to for BEEHIVE OF FUN:
Draw a BEEHIVE for the children to see. Then under it write *BEE kind*. They must think of as many *Bees* as they can add that would please Jesus. Let them read their lists at the end of three minutes of brainstorming.

SS895

THE GREAT DIVIDE

Time involved: Five minutes

Supplies: Large chalkboard, chalk for each student.

Purpose: To allow the children to express publicly how they came to Christ, how God answered prayer, or how they witness, etc.

How-to for THE GREAT DIVIDE:
With a piece of chalk, divide the chalkboard into enough sections for students to have their own private sections. Tell them to write out the subject chosen for the day. The students must write at least three sentences, but not more than five. Save the words until the end of class and read the testimonies to the rest of the class. The teacher can read, one student can read for the other students, or each one can read his own.

SS895

MY DESCRIPTION

Time involved: Four minutes

Supplies: Scrap paper, pencils, worktable.

Purpose: To let the students find out how great they are in God's sight. "It is He that hath made us, not we ourselves;" (Psalm 100:3 KJV).

How-to for MY DESCRIPTION:
Give students pieces of paper and pencils. Explain that they must describe themselves in ten to fifteen words, no more, no less. Let students read their own descriptions, or the teacher can read them and let the students guess who is being described. Add that each person is unique and very special in God's sight.

PYRAMID WRITING

Time involved: Five minutes

Supplies: Papers (approximately 5½″ × 8″), pencils.

Purpose: To stimulate children's imaginations and to focus minds on the subject of the day.

How-to for PYRAMID WRITING:
Hand out paper with lines drawn on it. Children are to write sentences with one word, then two words, then three words, etc., on the given subject of the day. This is a good way to review the previous lesson and set the tone for the new lesson.
Example for Zacchaeus:

STOP!
Look down.
Listen to Jesus.
Jump down from tree.
Ask Jesus to forgive me.
Begin to live a new life.

HOW WOULD YOU ACT? FILL IN THE LINES.

SS895

MY WILL

Time involved: Five minutes

Supplies: Paper with fancy borders and the words *My Last Will and Testament* printed across the top, copier, pens, scrap paper.

Purpose: To allow the children to realize life isn't unending. They have to think about life after death.

How-to for MY WILL:

Give the children copies of the MY WILL paper and tell them to write out how they would want their possessions distributed in case of their deaths. Have students practice on scrap paper, because there is only one fancy sheet per student. Perhaps they could consider giving away things other than material items. For example, jokes, their disposition, their helpfulness. Let them read their WILLS at the end of the class time.

My Last Will and Testament

I give my joke-telling ability to Joe.

My bedroom to my sister.

My baseball cards to Hank.

signed—
Tommy Paine

IF YOU WERE TO DIE, HOW WOULD YOU GIVE AWAY YOUR THINGS?

IMAGINARY LETTER

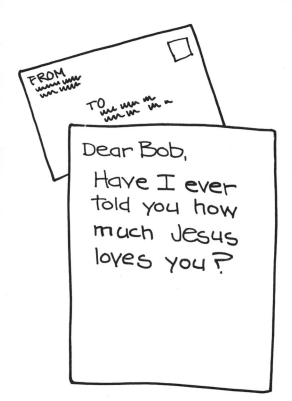

Dear Bob,
Have I ever told you how much Jesus loves you?

Time involved: Five minutes

Supplies: Writing paper, pens, envelopes.

Purpose: To see where the students are spiritually. These letters will let the teacher discover if the students understand the Gospel and if they are serious about witnessing.

How-to for IMAGINARY LETTER:
Show a letter neatly written on stationery to the class. The teacher can write the letter to a friend who doesn't know the Lord. Then, give the students paper and envelopes and have them write a letter to an imaginary friend who doesn't know the Lord. They can use Bible verses and their own beliefs to invite their friends to become Christians. Let them sign their letters and seal them in envelopes. The teacher can collect the letters and answer each one the next week with suggestions and help. Perhaps someday they can write a real letter to a friend or relative inviting him to learn about Jesus.

WRITE TO AN IMAGINARY FRIEND.

Shining Star Publications, Copyright © 1991, A division of Good Apple   SS895

DOWN TIME

Time involved: Five minutes

Supplies: Copier paper, sample sheets, fine-tip felt pens, pencils or pens.

Purpose: To get the students concentrating on a Bible verse that is important to the lesson.

How-to for DOWN TIME:
Choose an important verse in the lesson. Write the first letter of each word across the top of the sample paper. Put lines for each letter that must be added. Include the Scripture reference and make a copy for each student. Give students four minutes to write out the verse and then have the class read it in unison. For example, John 14:2 will look like this:

```
I   M F H A M R ;   I I   W N S I   W H
—   — — — — — — —   — —   — — — —   — —
    — — — — — —       — —             — —
    — —   — —           — —            — —
    — —   —              —              —
    —
    —
```

```
T Y. I   A G T T P A P F Y.   J
— —       — — — — —   — — — —  o
— —       — —   —     — — —    h
—         — —   —       —      n
          — —   —       —
                —             14:
                —              2
```

SS895

CHECK-WRITING SKILLS

Time involved: Four minutes

Supplies: Discontinued checks or copier plus copied blank checks, scrap paper, pens or pencils.

Purpose: To help students make decisions regarding the Lord's work.

How-to for CHECK-WRITING SKILLS:

Prepare the checks with the word *void* printed on each one. Explain clearly that they can't be cashed. Then tell the students that they have an imaginary $100.00 to give to the Lord's work. On scrap paper, let them figure out what they will do with it. Explain some needs: the church and its needs, a poor family down the street, a missionary in Africa who needs funds for literature, a young couple trying to raise support to go to the mission field for the first time, the Sunday school. Explain that if they neglect the home church, no missionaries would ever be sent out. After several minutes, ask them how they spent their $100.00. Explain that there are no right or wrong answers; that in life, they should give as the Lord leads, as long as they do not neglect their own church. Then teach the lesson on giving.

Shining Star Publications, Copyright © 1991, A division of Good Apple

SS895

WHY, TEACHER?

Time involved: Five minutes

Supplies: Scrap paper, pens or pencils, chalkboard, chalk.

Purpose: To make the students think clearly and to help them understand the Bible for themselves.

How-to for WHY, TEACHER?:

Write a sample question on the chalkboard and then have the children each write a *why* question about a short portion of the Bible. If the Scripture portion is John 3:2, the sample *why* question could be: "Why did Nicodemus come to Jesus by night?" Let the students use open Bibles and write one *why* question on their scrap paper. After one minute, go around the class having each one ask his *why* question. But the teacher should say, "I want your opinions before I give mine." Let one or two students try; then the teacher can give a short answer. No long sermons are necessary, only a one sentence answer. This is just the opening to a more complete lesson on the subject.

CARD PICK

Time involved: Five or six minutes

Supplies: Reference books (dictionary, thesaurus), scrap paper, pencils, small cards (2″ × 4″).

Purpose: To practice using reference books.

How-to for CARD PICK:
Make two or three cards for each of these words: *Definition, Synonym, My Words, Question, How To,* and *Explanation.* Mix up the cards and pile them in the center of the table. Give each student a piece of paper and a pencil. Let each one take a card, look at a specific Bible word that will serve to introduce the lesson, and do what the card says. For example, the teacher might write the word *servant* on the board and allow students three minutes to find and write the answer to what was on the cards they drew. Let the students share their answers. Work on any misconceptions with Bible references during the lesson.

DEFINITION

SYNONYM

MY WORDS

QUESTION

HOW TO

EXPLANATION

YOU MAY USE THESE REFERENCE BOOKS.

DICTIONARY

THESAURUS

SS895

GAMES

HUNT AND FIND

Time involved: Four minutes

Supplies: Index cards (3" × 5"), pen.

Purpose: To bring excitement to the opening minutes of the Bible class.

How-to for HUNT AND FIND:
Before students arrive, print the Bible verse on a card. Hide the card in an inconspicuous place in the room. Be sure the card is visible from some angle. Say to the students, "Our Bible verse is here somewhere. Find the card it is written on. One, two, three, go!" The first child to find the card can present the verse to the other students, or help teach the verse to the class, or be scorekeeper in a Bible quiz, etc.

FIND THE CARD.

SS895

SNAP TO IT

Time involved: Five minutes

Supplies: A circle of chairs.

Purpose: To prepare a happy atmosphere for the Bible lesson.

How-to for SNAP TO IT:

Arrange the chairs in a circle and let the children sit wherever they desire. The teacher is IT for the first round. She can "snap" her fingers and say a letter that will begin a biblical name. She points to a student who must snap his fingers, say the original letter, and add a letter. If he hesitates more than three seconds, he is out. When he adds a letter, he must have a biblical name in mind. He then points to another student who must snap her fingers, add a letter and point to a fourth student. Game continues until a biblical name has been spelled out. The person who finishes the name may be IT and start a new biblical name. Play several times. After each round, those who are "out" can come back into the game. After five minutes go into the lesson of the day.

SS895

UNDER THE TABLE

Time involved: Five minutes

Supplies: A table, chairs around it, a beanbag or substitute.

Purpose: To make the opening moments a happy time and to guide the students into a happy Bible study.

How-to for UNDER THE TABLE:

Arrange the students evenly around the table so that they can easily reach the hand of the next person. Explain the rules: the beanbag is to be passed under the table person to person. When the teacher claps his hands, the student holding the beanbag must call out a Bible book. Continue passing the beanbag. When the teacher claps his hands again, another Bible book must be called out by the student holding the beanbag. No Bible books can be renamed. Be sure the students pass the beanbag quickly. The teacher will not be able to see who has the beanbag, so he cannot be accused of clapping unfairly. Keep going for not more than five minutes. All those who have not missed three times are declared the winners.

SS895

THREE BY THREE

Time involved: Five or six minutes

Supplies: Cardboard square (3' × 3'), wide-tip felt markers, table to play on, two different colored crayons.

Purpose: To allow for needed competition and to lead into a Bible study.

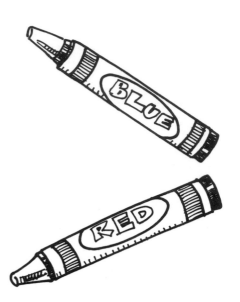

How-to for THREE BY THREE:

Make a gameboard. Divide the square cardboard into nine equal squares as shown in the illustration. Make a list of questions about previous lessons. Divide the class into two teams. Ask team one a question. If they answer it correctly in three seconds, they color in any square. If they miss, the question goes to the other team. If they answer correctly, they color in a square. The teams get 100 points for each square they have colored in and 200 points extra for every line of squares they have at the end of the game (vertical, horizontal, or diagonal). The team with the most points is declared the winner.

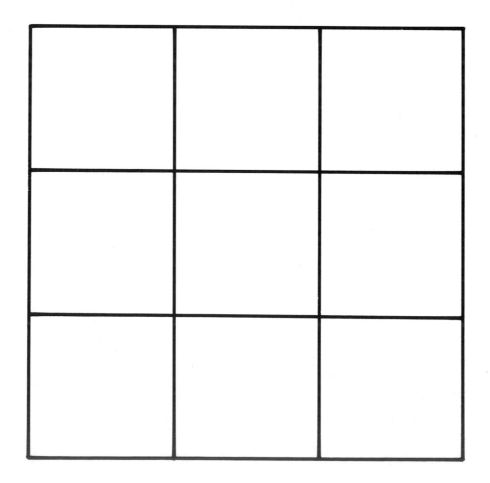

TABLE TAG

Time involved: Five minutes

Supplies: A table for the students to sit around.

Purpose: To provide excitement and fun while reviewing the Bible books.

How-to for TABLE TAG:

Explain the rules of TABLE TAG. A student is chosen to be IT. IT can tag any student, but he must call out a Bible book at the same time. The tagged student must call out the book that comes after the book IT mentioned. If the person that was tagged doesn't answer correctly, she becomes IT. If the tagged person does answer correctly, IT remains IT and calls out a different Bible book and tags another student. Continue play for five minutes and use the game again another day.

SS895

ROLL-A-THON

Time involved: Five minutes

Supplies: Corrugated cardboard, wide-tip felt marker, sharp scissors, marbles.

Purpose: To make the opening of the class period interesting and challenging.

How-to for ROLL-A-THON:
Cut three circles out of the corrugated cardboard. Label the holes: 1) Name a Bible book: 100 points; 2) Quote a Bible verse: 200 points; 3) Name a Bible character we have studied this year: 300 points. Give each student a marble and tell him to roll the marble on the board from the starting point and do what the circle it lands in says. If the marble doesn't go into a circle, the student gets another try for half the points. If the student misses that time, he waits until his next turn. Each student can have two turns. The one with the most points is the winner.

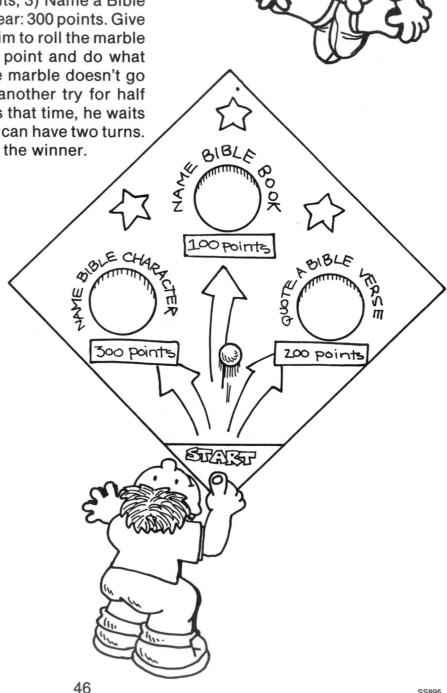

SS895

THE BIBLE SAYS

Time involved: Four minutes

Supplies: Space in front of each child's chair.

Purpose: To have an informal opening that is both fun and helpful.

How-to for THE BIBLE SAYS:
The teacher is the leader, at least for the first few times. The leader will say something like this list of actions:

1) The Bible says to hurt others
2) The Bible says to love
3) The Bible says to sing
4) The Bible says to cheat
5) The Bible says to lie
6) The Bible says to hate
7) The Bible says to help others
8) The Bible says to pray

Every time the leader says something that is false, the students are to stamp their feet. Every time the teacher says something that is correct, the students are to clap their hands.

THE BIBLE SAYS TO HATE.

THE BIBLE SAYS TO PRAY.

SS895

COPY BUG

Time involved: Four minutes

Supplies: Space in front of students' chairs.

Purpose: To have fun and let children use their physical agility.

How-to for COPY BUG:

The teacher can have a Bible action word in mind like L-O-V-E. She can start an action of her choice. For example, she would say "L" and put her hand on her hip. The student to her left must stand and do the teacher's action, add an action of his own (such as cock his head to the right) and say the second letter. The next student in the circle does the previous actions plus a new one and adds the next letter of the Bible action word. The next student in the circle stands, performs all the actions, adds a new one and says the final letter. Then the next student begins a new Bible action word. Do two or three Bible action words before plunging into the lesson.

SS895

FINGER SOCCER

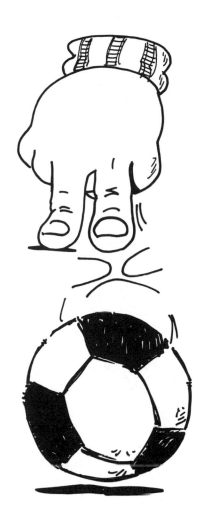

Time involved: Five minutes

Supplies: Tennis ball, felt-tip markers, large card-board (at least 18" × 24"), extra cardboard for circles.

Purpose: To utilize a fun game to introduce a serious Bible subject.

How-to for FINGER SOCCER:

Draw soccer ball markings with a felt-tip marker on a tennis ball. To make a gameboard from the large cardboard, cut out several circles; then glue larger circles under the holes for the "soccer ball" to roll into. A student can push, snap or roll the "soccer ball" toward any circle. If it stops in a circle, he must do what that circle says.

Circle 1: Tell what you like best about the Christian life.
Circle 2: Repeat a Bible verse from memory.
Circle 3: Tell what you find the hardest about living a Christian life.
Circle 4: Share a favorite Bible story.
Circle 5. Share a blessing or a prayer request.

Let each student have two turns. Save the game to play again in a month or two.

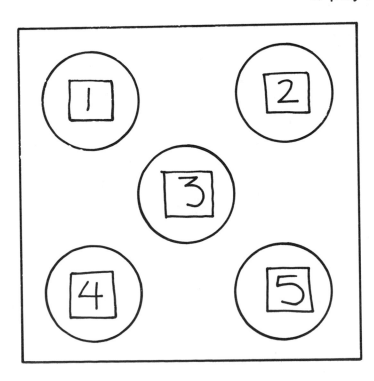

DO WHAT IT SAYS.

SS895

NO SMILE

Time involved: Four minutes

Supplies: Space for a circle of chairs without a table in the middle.

Purpose: To allow the students to enjoy the fun of a game and to learn a few Bible facts.

How-to for NO SMILE:

Have the children sit on chairs in a circle. Choose someone to be IT. IT must sit in the center of the circle and be prepared to ask a question. If the teacher wants the students to remember the books of the Bible in order, the game can be based on Bible books. IT goes to a student in the circle, squats and says, "Luke." IT can smile, make a face or giggle (but not touch the student); the one facing IT must say the name of the next Bible book without smiling. The teacher can be the judge of a smile. If the student can answer, "After Luke comes John," without smiling, IT remains IT; but, if the student smiles or giggles or makes a mistake, he becomes IT. Game continues.

A variation could be for IT to say, "Give me one Bible miracle," while squatting before a student. The student must answer with a miracle by saying, "A Bible miracle is the feeding of the five thousand," without smiling. If he can't say a correct answer without a smile, he is IT. If he can, IT goes to another student.

SS895

ONLY THREE

Time involved: Five minutes

Supplies: Scrap paper, pencils, table.

Purpose: To review past lessons and to give children a happy beginning for lessons of the day.

How-to for ONLY THREE:

Distribute the scrap paper and pencils and assure the students that they do not have to work hard for this *quiz*. They only need three answers to each question. The quiz could be to list three of each of the following:

1. disciples
2. Old Testament books
3. prophets
4. Paul's letters
5. verses from memory
6. miracles
7. New Testament books
8. plagues
9. Ten Commandments
10. fruit of the Spirit

After the students finish (four minutes), correct their answers and go on into the lesson.

GIVE 3 ANSWERS TO EACH QUESTION.

SS895

SITTING RELAY

Time involved: Five minutes

Supplies: 2 strong, inexpensive, long necklaces, 3" × 5" cards, table with chairs along each side.

Purpose: To review information that will help the students prepare for a new lesson.

How-to for SITTING RELAY:
Prepare questions that the students should know the answers to and that would set the stage for a new lesson. If the class had been studying the life of Jesus, the questions might include:

Where was Jesus born?
Where had Jesus gone when his parents couldn't find Him?
To whom did Jesus say, "I will make you fishers of men"?
Which disciple was the brother of Andrew?
What special miracle did Jesus do in Bethany?
What miracle did Jesus do in Cana?

Write each question on a 3" × 5" card. Hand student #1 on each team a necklace. Place a set of questions on the table by each team. Each student must put on the necklace, pick up a question, answer it correctly, take off the necklace, and hand it to the next student, who then must put it on, take a question and answer it correctly, take off the necklace and pass it to the next student. The first team to get through their line is the winning team. Answered questions should be placed on the bottom of the pack to be used a second time. If a question is missed, the teacher must give the correct answer and the team must start from the beginning again.

QUESTION BOWL

Time involved: Four or five minutes

Supplies: Small cards, pen, large glass bowl.

Purpose: To give the students an opportunity to compete and recall information from previous lessons.

How-to for QUESTION BOWL:

Write out Bible names from the content of recent lessons. Add a score, such as 20, 30, 40, 50, depending on how obscure the name is. Fold the cards in half and place them in the bowl. Make enough questions to allow each student two or three turns. One at a time, children take turns picking a card from the bowl. Choose a scorekeeper. The first child must tell who the person is that is named on the card she drew. If she is correct, she gets the number of points listed on the card. The teacher is the judge. If the student is partially right, the teacher can award her half or a quarter of the points. The individual student with the highest score is the winner. Play for five minutes and reward the winner with a small gift.

CANDY HUNT

Time involved: Four minutes

Supplies: Individually wrapped candies, paper, pen, cellophane tape.

Purpose: To make the opening few minutes both exciting and rewarding.

How-to for CANDY HUNT:
Write out about twenty questions on paper in small print. Cut them apart and attach them to the candies with cellophane tape. Before class, hide them around the classroom. At the strike of ten o'clock (or whatever the starting time), explain that the students are to find as many candies as they can. They must answer the question in order to keep the candy. If they can't answer the question, the teacher keeps the candy for another time, or helps the student until a proper answer is obtained. Examples:

1) Who was Cain's father?
2) Who was Joseph's father?
3) Who was John the Baptist's father?
4) Who was John the disciple's father?
5) Who was Absolom's father?
6) Who was Isaac's father?
7) Who was Ham's father?
8) Who was Jesus' father?

The questions can be opinion questions. Examples:
1) Why should we pray?
2) Why should we come to Bible class?
3) Why should we tell others about Jesus?
4) Why should we read the Bible?
5) Why should we believe in Jesus?
6) Why should we follow the commandments?
7) Why should we pay attention in class?
8) Why should we memorize Bible verses?

COUNT OFF

WHAT WAS PAUL'S FORMER NAME?

SAUL

Time involved: Five minutes

Supplies: Circle of chairs (around table or separate).

Purpose: Review past lessons and introduce new concepts.

How-to for COUNT OFF:

Make a list of questions for the class. Twenty would probably be enough. If the class is studying the life of Paul, questions might include:

1) What was Paul's former name?
2) Where was Paul born?
3) Who did God use to bring back Paul's eyesight?
4) Where did Paul go after he left Damascus?
5) How did Paul escape from Damascus?

Or, you could use: If you were Paul . . .

1) How would you react on the road to Damascus?
2) How would you treat John Mark?
3) How would you feel when you met Ananias?
4) How would you feel as you entered Jerusalem for the first time after you came to Christ?
5) What would you do after you were stoned in Lystra?

Start with the student on your left. He becomes "one" and counts out loud. The one next to him says "two," etc. When someone says "seven," that student must answer a question. Then the student next to him is "eight" and the counting continues. Every time someone calls out "seven," a number divisible by seven, or a number containing the numeral seven (like 27), that student must answer a question. Continue for five minutes. The suspense and interest will remain high throughout the entire game.

SS895

VERSE FORWARD

Time involved: Five or six minutes

Supplies: Chalk or string to mark a start and finish line.

Purpose: To help the children hide God's Word, the Bible, in their hearts.

How-to for VERSE FORWARD:

Mark a start and a finish line. Line up the students at the start line and let the one on the left be number one. Count off; ask the children to remember their numbers. Starting with number one, the first child must tell a Bible verse from memory. If the child does it correctly, she can take one giant step toward the finish line. If it is said almost perfectly she can take one regular step. If she can say only part of a verse, one baby step may be taken. Then child number two can try. It must be a different verse. He advances by the same regulations. The first student to reach the finish line is declared the winner.

I WILL, I WON'T

Time involved: Five minutes

Supplies: A circle of chairs.

Purpose: To have an informal beginning to class and to let the teacher have some insights into the students' needs.

How-to for I WILL, I WON'T:

Choose a student to be IT or the teacher can be IT for the first time. IT points to any student, addresses her by name and says, "I will," or "I won't." For example: "Jane, I will," or, "Jane, I won't—one, two, three." Before IT gets to three, Jane must begin answering with an "I will" or "I won't" statement. For instance, if IT said, "I won't," Jane might answer: "I won't pray" or "I won't go to church," etc. The "I will" answers are to be actions that will please the Lord. The "I won't" answers are to be actions that will not please the Lord. If the student doesn't start the answer by the count of three, she becomes IT. If the child does begin the answer by the count of three, IT must go to another student. Vary the order of "I will" or "I won't." If a child answers with an "I will" when he was supposed to give an "I won't," he becomes IT. The students who never become IT (except the first one who was chosen to begin the game) are declared the winners.

Shining Star Publications, Copyright © 1991, A division of Good Apple.

PUZZLES

VOWEL MYSTERY

Time involved: Four or five minutes

Supplies: Paper, copier, pencils or pens.

Purpose: To make the opening moments both challenging and fun-filled.

How-to for VOWEL MYSTERY:
Choose a phrase from a Bible verse or an aim in the Bible lesson and print it without its vowels. Hand a copy of the verse to the students and allow them three or four minutes to complete the verse. Be sure to let one child give the answer before plunging into the lesson. For example, "Come unto me . . ." will look like this:

"C __ M __   __ N T __   M __ . . ."

ELONGATED BOOKS

Time involved: Five or six minutes

Supplies: Copier, copier paper, pencils.

Purpose: To help the students learn the names and spellings of the books of the Bible.

How-to for ELONGATED BOOKS:

Explain the rules to the students. Starting with a Bible book printed on their papers, students must add other books of the Bible to it, up, down or sideways. The Bible index will help them. The addition must be a Bible book that begins or ends with the last letter of the previous book listed. The student who can include the most Bible books will win. There are several ways to do the puzzle. If one book leads to a dead end, the student can erase that name and try another book.

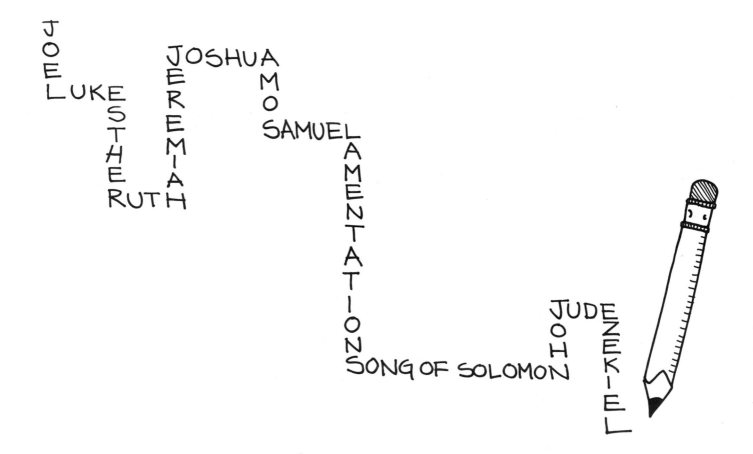

ADVANCE THREE

Time involved: Five minutes

Supplies: Copier or carbon paper, paper, pencils.

Purpose: To introduce a new Bible verse in a challenging way.

How-to for ADVANCE THREE:

Select a Bible verse that will be helpful for the presentation of the lesson. If the subject is fear, John 14:27 might be a good verse. Tell the students to try to decode the verse for themselves. After several minutes, tell them that every letter given is alphabetically three letters beyond the one needed in the blank. Example:

D O   N O T   L E T   Y O U R   H E A R T
G R   Q R W   O H W   B R X U   K H D U W

B E   T R O U B L E D   A N D   D O
E H   W U R X E O H G   D Q G   G R

N O T   B E   A F R A I D
Q R W   E H   D I U D L G

Allow about five minutes to complete the puzzle and be sure the correct answer is given. Another time, let them write a Bible verse using the ADVANCE THREE code.

ADVANCE 3 TO FIGURE IT OUT.

SS895

PICTURE PUZZLE

Time involved: Five minutes

Supplies: Plain white paper, Bibles, pencils or pens.

Purpose: To allow the students to become more familiar with the Bible and to memorize specific verses.

How-to for PICTURE PUZZLE:
Give the Scripture reference that goes with the lesson of the day. Let the students locate it in their Bibles and copy it on their papers. As they copy, the letters must make a shape that will represent the verse. For example, if the verse is John 3:16, the verse could be written in the shape of the world or the shape of a heart. If the verse is Psalm 23:1, the picture could be the shape of a sheep. Let them use their imaginations. A variation of PICTURE PUZZLE could be to give the students different verses, let them follow these directions, and when their verses come up in the lesson, have them read the verse and share their drawings with the class.

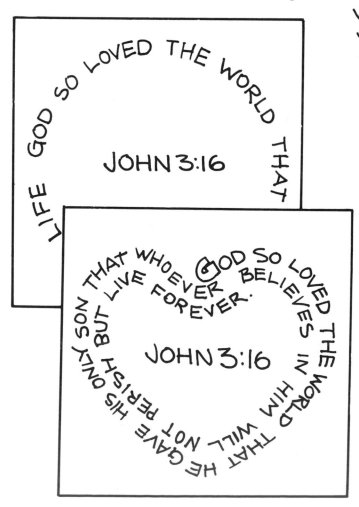

WRITE YOUR VERSE IN A PICTURE SHAPE.

SS895

HIDDEN VERSE

CIRCLE EVERY WORD.

Time involved: Five minutes

Supplies: Copier and copier paper, or paper, ball point pen and carbon paper, Bibles.

Purpose: To stretch the curiosity and the imaginations of the students and to increase their Bible knowledge.

How-to for HIDDEN VERSE:
Select a Bible verse to be memorized or studied and turn it into a puzzle. Type the verse with extra letters between words and without spaces. If the verse is Matthew 28:19, it might look like this:

WERTTHEREFOREYUIGOOPASDANDFGJMAKEKLZ

HSDGDISCIPLESVBNMNHTOFQSCVDWALLRTFGH

NATIONSKEDCIFBAPTIZINGRYGJIHGTHEMSDG

JORTINVNHETHESFHNAMEQETUIJGVOFQFBJUG

FIUNTHEQZFUNKFATHERSFHBANDSFWTUOFCVG

TFDSTHEQDBUJJSONADGJGDEANDOFQJDFVBJG

CGYKOTHEKFODOXICHOLYSFHMNXDFOSPIRITG

If the verse for the day is I Peter 5:7, it might look like this:

FJGDCASTQETUIPALLTGBNHYJMYOURFGADHK

KANXIETYCFGHYONMKOIJNBHIMFREDCVDGKJ

FJHBECAUSEMIYUPHEDHSJAKSLCARESMWOIU

WSXCDERFVBGFORMKHJHHGFYOUQETUOPIYRW

Give the children the reference and let them circle each correct word in the puzzle.

SS895

MYSTERIOUS WORDS

Time involved: Five or six minutes

Supplies: Copier, copy paper, or typewriter, carbon paper and typing paper, pencils, Bibles.

Purpose: To stretch the minds of the students and help them increase their Bible research skills.

FIND OUR BIBLE VERSE.

How-to for MYSTERIOUS WORDS:

Select a phrase or Bible verse that will help in the teaching of the lesson. Give different Scripture references for each word in the phrase or the verse. Let the students find it via directions and an open Bible. If the phrase to be remembered is from John 15:17, "This is my command: love each other," these directions would be appropriate:

1) Second word in
   John 16:1   _____
2) First word in
   John 18:34   _____
3) Seventh word in
   John 15:1   _____
4) Last word in
   John 15:14   _____
5) Third word in
   John 14:15   _____
6) Sixth word in
   John 15:12   _____
7) Seventeenth word in
   John 21:2   _____

Give the students time to find each word.

SS895

YOUR ABC's

Time involved: Five minutes

Supplies: Paper, copier or carbon paper, pencils.

Purpose: To make a statement in a fun way.

How-to for YOUR ABC's:
Select a phrase that could be the aim of the lesson. It could be, "I can read my own Bible every day," "I will try to obey my parents today," or, "With God's help, I will tell others about Jesus." Then eliminate all the A's, B's, and C's and challenge the students to figure out the statement. Example:

I _ _N R E _ D MY OWN

_ I _ L E EVERY D _ Y.

Give the students two minutes to complete the sentence; discuss it and pray for help in carrying out the phrase.

ALL ABC'S ARE MISSING.

SS895

MIRROR IMAGE VERSES

Time involved: Four minutes

Supplies: Copier, paper, typewriter, black carbon paper, pencils.

Purpose: To begin a Bible lesson in a challenging and fun way.

How-to for MIRROR IMAGE VERSES:
To create a master for a verse written backwards, place a piece of black carbon paper facing the backside of a sheet of paper and type the verse on the other side. As the keys strike the paper, the carbon will print the mirror image of the verse on the other side of the paper. Use the carbon side of the paper as a master and copy enough puzzles for each member of your class. Allow four to five minutes for students to decode the verse written backwards.

SS895

NUMBER CHART

Time involved: Five or six minutes

Supplies: Copy of number chart and puzzle for each child, pencils.

Purpose: To make the students think and put a chosen Bible verse in their minds.

How-to for NUMBER CHART:

Using the grid code found below, write out the chosen Bible verse in number code. Example: 1, 4 = D; 3, 5 = O. The first number indicates the row, and the second number indicates the column.

	1	2	3	4	5
1	A	B	C	D	E
2	F	G	H	I	J
3	K	L	M	N	O
4	P	Q	R	S	T
5	U	V	W	X	Y

(0, 0 = Z)

Puzzle code for John 3:16a (KJV)

2,1	3,5	4,3	_____				
2,2	3,5	1,4	_____				
4,4	3,5	_____					
3,2	3,5	5,2	1,5	1,4	_____		
4,5	2,3	1,5	_____				
5,3	3,5	4,3	3,2	1,4	_____		
4,5	2,3	1,1	4,5	_____			
2,3	1,5	_____					
2,2	1,1	5,2	1,5	_____			
2,3	2,4	4,4	_____				
3,5	3,4	3,2	5,5	_____			
1,2	1,5	2,2	3,5	4,5	4,5	1,5	3,4	_____
4,4	3,5	3,4	_____				

SS895

TWO BY TWO

Time involved: Five minutes

Supplies: Paper, pencils, copier, typewriter, carbon
paper.

Purpose: To encourage the students to think and to
memorize a Bible verse.

How-to for TWO BY TWO:
Copy the puzzle found below or make up one of
your own. Every other word goes together to make
up the first verse; then every other word not used
in the first verse makes up the words in the second
verse. The verses hidden in this puzzle are Isaiah
25:1a and Isaiah 26:4.

```
O T R U S T L O R D I N Y O U
  T H E A R E L O R D M Y
  F O R E V E R G O D F O R I
T H E W I L L L O R D E X A L T
  T H E Y O U L O R D A N D
  I S P R A I S E T H E Y O U R
  R O C K N A M E E T E R N A L
I S A I A H I S A I A H 2 5 : 1a ; 2 6 : 4
```

EVERY OTHER
WORD IS...

Allow the students about four minutes to write out
the verses correctly. Let them read the verses and
memorize one.

SS895

CROSSWORD VERSE

Time involved: Five minutes

Supplies: Paper, pencils, copier or carbon paper.

Purpose: To make the learning of a Bible verse fun and easy.

How-to for CROSSWORD VERSE:

Make up a puzzle like the one shown here or use this one from Isaiah 25:8a. Give the students four minutes to figure out the verse and one minute to memorize it.

			1			2
	3			4		
5						
6						

1) down-3rd word   3) across-5th word
2) down-6th word   5) across-2nd word
4) down-1st word   6) across-4th word

Answer
Key:

```
X  X  X  S  X  X  X  F
X  X  X  W  X  X  X  O
X  D  E  A  T  H  X  R
X  X  X  L  X  E  X  E
W  I  L  L  X  X  X  V
X  X  X  O  X  X  X  E
U  P  X  W  X  X  X  R
```

WRITE DOWN

Time involved: Four or five minutes

Supplies: Copier or carbon paper, paper, pencils.

Purpose: To make the students think and get involved with a subject that will introduce the lesson of the day.

How-to for WRITE DOWN:

In large letters, write an appropriate word across the top of each student's paper. Instruct the students to choose words about the subject that begin with each letter of the word. For example, if the chosen word is *Bible*, the children are to list five words associated with the Bible. The first word will begin with the letter B, the second word will begin with the letter I, the third will begin with the letter B, etc. If the chosen word is *prayer*, children are to list six words associated with prayer, each one beginning with a different letter in the word *prayer*. After three minutes, let each child share his acrostic word list.

Shining Star Publications, Copyright © 1991, A division of Good Apple

SS895

FOUR-LETTER WORD HUNT

Time involved: Five minutes

Supplies: Two large pieces of paper, two pencils.

Purpose: To make the students work together in groups and to think about words and their meaning.

How-to for FOUR-LETTER WORD HUNT:
Explain the rules of the puzzle to the students. Divide the students into two teams. They are to think of a four-letter word that has something to do with the subject of the day. If the students are learning about the life of Jesus, the words could be: *pray, come, love, help, John*, etc. They must write their words on their papers but not let the other team see their words. Choose one team to begin. They call out a letter they think their opponents may have in their word. The other team says "yes" or "no." Then they choose a letter they think is in their opponent's word. The calling out of letters goes on until one team can guess the other team's word. The team that does so first is the winner.

CHOOSE A 4-LETTER WORD.

LOVE

SS895

BIBLE VERSE ADDITION

Time involved: Four minutes

Supplies: Chalkboard, eraser, chalk.

Purpose: To learn a significant Bible verse that will help in the study of the lesson.

How-to for BIBLE VERSE ADDITION:
Let the children look at the Bible verse printed on the chalkboard. Let student number one say the first word. The second student must say the first word and add the second word. The third student must say the first and second words and add the third word. The verse keeps getting repeated until the entire verse is said. Then let the teacher erase the chalkboard and start again. This time the students must do it from memory.

SS895

MUSICAL LETTERS

Time involved: Five or six minutes

Supplies: Poster paper or chalkboard, copier paper, pencils.

Purpose: To make the students think about a Scripture and have fun.

How-to for MUSICAL LETTERS:
Draw the musical notes and their letter equivalents on the chalkboard or poster board. Make a sheet with the verse in musical notes only and have it copied. Give one to each student and let them figure out the verse. Then, in silence, let them memorize it and share the verse with the class.

Key:

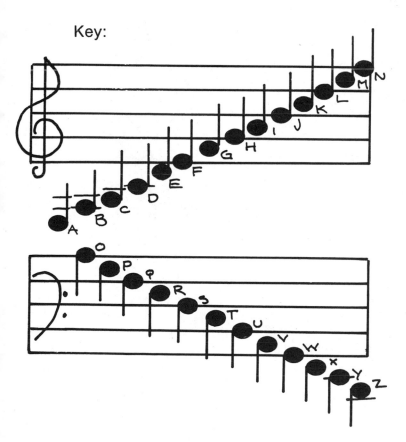

Example:

*Teachers: These notes are for fun, not to teach musically correct notations.

CAN YOU FIND TEN?

Time involved: Four or five minutes

Supplies: Paper, pencils.

Purpose: To help the students center their minds on a particular subject and figure out words from one big word.

How-to for CAN YOU FIND TEN?:

Ask each student to write the chosen word on their paper. If the lesson is on Jesus' death on the cross, use *salvation*; if the lesson is on how God made the world, use *Creation*; if the lesson is on the life of Christ, use *discipleship*. The rules are: think of words that can be made from the letters in the chosen word. Each letter can be used only as many times as it is found in the chosen word. Letters may be reused in the next word. Each word must have at least three letters. They must find ten words. Time limit is four minutes. The student who is the first to write down ten words reads her list to the rest of the class. Repeat the main word and plunge into the subject!

FIND 10 WORDS.

SALVATION

SS895

ENDS

Time involved: Five minutes

Supplies: Chalkboard, chalk, paper, pencils.

Purpose: To help the students remember the books of the Bible.

How-to for ENDS:
On the chalkboard, ask for the following:

Five Bible books ending in IAH
Five Bible books ending in IANS
Five Bible books ending in S
Five Bible books ending in L

Allow the students four minutes. After two minutes they can look in their Bibles if they can't remember. They get fifty (50) points for those they remember without their Bibles and twenty-five (25) points for those they find by using their Bibles.

SS895

THREE TIMES AS NICE

Time involved: Four or five minutes

Supplies: Pen, copier, paper, pencils.

Purpose: To see how quickly the students can write out the Bible verse of the day. Let them learn it or put it into their own words when they finish.

How-to for THREE TIMES AS NICE:
Choose a verse that is important to the lesson. Write it out on paper and copy it, one per student. Let them figure out the verse and write it correctly. Then have them memorize it or put it into their own words.

PPPSSSAAALLLMMM 111111999:::888999

YYYOOOUUURRR WWWOOORRRDDD,,,
OOO LLLOOORRRDDD,,, IIISSS
EEETTTEEERRRNNNAAALLL;;;
IIITTT SSSTTTAAANNNDDDSSS
FFFIIIRRRMMM IIINNN TTTHHHEEE
HHHEEEAAAVVVEEENNNSSS...

WHAT'S THE VERSE?

SS895

THREE-CHOICE QUESTIONS

Time involved: Five minutes

Supplies: Copier or carbon paper, typewriter paper, pencils, typewriter.

Purpose: To center the students' minds on the subject of the day and to test their knowledge on the subject.

How-to for THREE-CHOICE QUESTIONS:

Type out ten questions that will introduce the subject of the lesson study. If the day's lesson is on knowing Christ as Savior and Lord, the questions might be:

1) Heaven is for
    a) good people   b) bad people
    c) people who believe in Jesus

2) Jesus died
    a) to take away sin   b) because He was old
    c) to punish Him for His own sins

3) Jesus died in
    a) Bethlehem   b) Nazareth   c) Golgotha

4) To know Jesus, we must
    a) read the Bible   b) go to church
    c) receive Him into our lives

5) Jesus said
    a) "Come unto Me . . ."
    b) "Believe Buddha . . ."
    c) "Trust in Mohammed . . ."

6) Jesus' words about salvation are in the
    a) Bible   b) encyclopedia   c) Koran

7) We are forgiven of our sins when
    a) we read our Bibles   b) we confess
    c) we tell the pastor

8) God chose Jesus to die because
    a) He was young   b) He was sinless
    c) He was a good man

9) When we become Christians
    a) we go right to heaven
    b) we can't sin anymore
    c) we become God's child

10) Christians are people who
    a) aren't Jews   b) don't swear
    c) believe in Jesus

Give the students three minutes to answer (if needed) and then go over each question. Be sure to give the right answer and to explain any questions the children may have.

SS895

SCRIPTURE SEARCH AND STORYTELLING

SS895

ONLY THREE

Time involved: Five minutes

Supplies: Paper, pencils, copier or carbon paper.

Purpose: To stimulate thinking and interest.

How-to for ONLY THREE:
Give each student a paper with the list of threes needed. Allow them three and one-half minutes to complete the "test"; then correct it so that they can find out their personal abilities and receive commendation for a job well done.

WRITE ONLY THREE.

Three disciples— 1. _____ 2. _____
    3. _____
Three miracles— 1. _____ 2. _____
    3. _____
Three Old Testament books— 1. _____
    2. _____ 3. _____
Three New Testament books— 1. _____
    2. _____ 3. _____
Three prophets— 1. _____ 2. _____
    3. _____
Three plagues— 1._____ 2._____
    3. _____
Three of Paul's Epistles— 1. _____
    2. _____ 3. _____
Three fruits of the Spirit— 1._____
    2. _____ 3. _____
Three verses from memory—
    1._____
    2._____
    3._____
Three commandments— 1. _____
    2._____ 3._____

Shining Star Publications, Copyright © 1991, A division of Good Apple

SS895

COLORING STORY

Time involved: Five minutes

Supplies: Pictures about the story to be shared, copier or carbon paper, crayons or pencil crayons, tape recorder.

Purpose: To occupy the students' hands during the tape recorded story and to help them focus their attention.

How-to for COLORING STORY:

Use a commercial tape recording of a Bible story or read one onto a tape. It should be about a four-minute story. Give the children pictures to be colored during the playing of the tape. There must be no talking, no moving, no noise during the few minutes needed. At the end of the tape, let them show their pictures and compliment each one.

TELEGRAMS

Time involved: Four or five minutes

Supplies: Paper, pencils.

Purpose: To make the students use their abilities in word power and write their thoughts on a subject.

How-to for TELEGRAMS:

Select a subject that would make an appropriate introduction to the lesson. If the lesson is on the Ten Commandments, the subject of the TELE-GRAM might be: "Why should I obey?" If the lesson is on Jesus' miracles, the subject of the TELEGRAM might be: "Why can't I do impossible acts?" Give each student paper and a pencil. Each one must write exactly ten words about the subject; it should make sense, but it doesn't have to be in complete sentences.

SS895

BEAT THE CLOCK

Time involved: Five minutes

Supplies: Paper, pencils, timer, or clock with a second hand and a bell.

Purpose: To make the students think quickly as well as accurately and to let the teacher see what they think or believe.

How-to for BEAT THE CLOCK:

Bring a timer to class (a clock with a second hand and a bell can be a substitute). Write out the questions on separate cards and place them, face down, on the table. Let the students pick a question from the pile. Set the clock for 30 seconds and let one student write an answer to the top question. A good series of questions for BEAT THE CLOCK might be:

How to pray.
How to help parents.
How to study the Bible.
How to tell others about Jesus.
How to prepare for class.
How to invite others to church.

When the timer rings, the student must stop and the teacher can decide if she BEAT THE CLOCK. If a sincere effort was made, the student did BEAT THE CLOCK even if her answer was not the best.

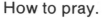

SS895

TODAY'S DRAMA

Time involved: Five or six minutes

Supplies: Space for stage.

Purpose: To let the students use their acting talents and show some of their inner views.

How-to for TODAY'S DRAMA:

Write out several acting subjects on papers and fold them in half. Let two or three students work as a team. The team chooses a paper and pantomimes what is on it. Give them one minute to prepare and one minute to perform. There can be imaginary props and the students can talk or sing or whatever they need to do. Suggested subjects for TODAY'S DRAMA are:

How to handle a parent who doesn't understand.
How to tell a friend how to become a Christian.
How to handle a student who tries to get you to try drugs.
How to find time to read the Bible and pray at home.

SS895

CARTOON STORY

Time involved: Five minutes

Supplies: Paper (8½" × 11"), pencils.

Purpose: To capitalize on the students' ability to draw and illustrate a subject.

How-to for CARTOON STORY:
Distribute the papers to the students and ask them to fold them in half, and in half again (resulting in quarters or four equal-sized areas to draw in). Let them go around each section with their pencils or markers. Then tell them to draw a cartoon story about a subject that would help them understand the story to be taught. Suggested topics are:

How to find the book of Ephesians in the Bible.
How to hide from God.
What happens to a new student in class.
If I were a missionary in the jungle . . .

Allow about three minutes to draw and two minutes to explain the cartoons.

SS895

STAND UP

Time involved: Four or five minutes

Supplies: Space in front of each chair to stand and turn around.

Purpose: To teach students to pay attention and listen while they learn.

How-to for STAND UP:
The teacher should tell a story about the subject of the day (not a Bible story, but something that could be funny, silly or informative). Every time the teacher uses the word *and* every student must stand, turn around, and sit down again. The teacher might want to tell a story about:

A child learning to pray
A student doing homework
A class member writing a letter to a missionary
A teacher getting ready for class

Let the story go on for about four minutes, and use *and* often.

 SS895

HOW DO YOU FEEL?

Time involved: Five minutes

Supplies: None.

Purpose: To help the students think about the subject and to voice their opinions.

How-to for HOW DO YOU FEEL?:
Choose a thought that would enter the students' minds on the subject of the day. If the lesson is on Jesus' miracles, the thought could be:

How would you feel if you saw Jesus heal a lame man?

If the lesson is on Moses leading the children of Israel, the thought could be:

How would you feel if you were following Moses?

Allow each child to say three sentences. They shouldn't copy each other. The statements ought to be original and meaningful. Do not criticize anyone's comments, but let them lead into the lesson.

IN ONLY 3 SENTENCES, TELL HOW YOU WOULD FEEL IF YOU WERE FOLLOWING MOSES.

I WOULD...

SS895

NO CRIME TO RHYME

Time involved: Five minutes

Supplies: Chalkboard, chalk, paper, pencils.

Purpose: To test the rhyming skills of the students and help them think of Bible characters that they have been studying.

How-to for NO CRIME TO RHYME:
Make a list of Bible people that have been used in recent lessons. Then, via your own thoughts, or through a rhyming dictionary, think of rhyming words. List the rhyming words on the chalkboard and ask the students to list the Bible characters that rhyme with those words. A list of people from Genesis could be:

Rhyming Words	Answers
1) RAM	(Abraham)
2) BACK	(Isaac)
3) HAM	(Adam)
4) LEAVE	(Eve)
5) LANE	(Cain)
6) DEAF	(Joseph)
7) RAW	(Esau)
8) VIA	(Leah)
9) CABLE	(Abel)
10) BIN	(Benjamin)

Allow the students three minutes to guess. Correct the papers together.

1 RAM
2 BACK
3 HAM
4 LEAVE
5 LANE
6 DEAF
7 RAW
8 VIA
9 CABLE
10 BIN

SS895

WHY?

Time involved: Five minutes

Supplies: None.

Purpose: To allow the students to have fun while learning a few facts or ideas.

How-to for WHY?:

The teacher should make up a story about real life, perhaps about a child the same age as the students. Let the imaginary character get up, read the Bible, pray, eat breakfast, clean his room, prepare for Bible class, and meet a friend. There can be complications, temptations, and delays. Select a *Pointer* from among the children. The *Pointer* is to point to a student every fifteen seconds. The student who was pointed at selects a good stopping place for the teacher's story and calls out "WHY." The teacher must answer WHY appropriately for the place she is in the story. For example, if she just said, "John ate oatmeal for breakfast," and the student said "WHY," the teacher would have to quickly answer, perhaps with "because it was good for him." Then the teacher would continue with the story until the next student asks "WHY." After four minutes, bring the story to a conclusion. Make the story relevant to the lesson.

SS895

VERSE ANSWERS

Time involved: Four or five minutes

Supplies: Small cards (3″ × 5″), marker.

Purpose: To help the students use the Bible to meet everyday needs.

How-to for VERSE ANSWERS:

Select four or five verses that the students have been learning in recent weeks. Write them on 3″ × 5″ cards and give one to each student. Then give some questions and ask the students to see if the verses they are holding will meet the needs found in the questions. Suggested questions might be:

When I am afraid to be alone . . .
When I am upset . . .
When I don't feel like doing my homework . . .
When my friend doesn't want to be with me . . .
When someone I love is very sick . . .

Bible verses with answers could be: Proverbs 3:5, 6; Matthew 11:28; Philippians 4:13; John 15:17; Philippians 4:19.

MOTION STORY

Time involved: Five minutes

Supplies: Space in front of the students' chairs.

Purpose: To encourage close attention to the story.

How-to for MOTION STORY:
Have an introductory story to tell. Use a key word such as *therefore* often. When the teacher says *therefore*, the student to his left does a motion and everyone copies. The next time he says *therefore*, the student to the left of the student who chose the first motion changes to a different motion. The teacher ought to use the key word often so that the motions change often. Motions may include: clapping, touching the head, stamping the feet, swinging arms, wiggling fingers or wrists, etc. The children will think of more. Make sure everyone has one opportunity to select a motion and then conclude the story.

SS895

BACKUPS

Time involved: Four or five minutes

Supplies: Chalkboard, chalk, scrap paper, pencils.

Purpose: To help the students use their sharp minds and remember Scripture in the process.

How-to for BACKUPS:

Select the key verse or another important verse for the day. Write the letters of the first word backwards on the chalkboard. Allow five seconds for the students to guess the word. Do not give the answer. Erase the letters and write the second word backwards on the chalkboard and allow them just five seconds to guess the word. Let them write their words on scrap paper; when they finally get the words of the verse, let them read it, memorize it, and be ready to quote it during the lesson period.

 SS895

BLIND ART

Time involved: Four minutes

Supplies: Paper, pencils.

Purpose: To set the students' minds on the subject of the day in a fun-filled way.

How-to for BLIND ART:
Give the children pieces of paper and pencils. Tell them they must close their eyes and draw the subject the teacher chooses.

If the subject is:	Pictures might be:
feeding the 5000	a crowd of people
crossing the Red Sea	a wide river
the Creation	3 animals and 2 plants
the stoning of Stephen	a pile of rocks

Any picture that relates is good. Be sure the children keep their eyes closed; when the time limit is reached—usually one minute is enough—let them look and laugh. The teacher can make one and be willing to laugh at his work, too. Make the transfer from the picture to the lesson.

SS895

CONTINUOUS SENTENCES

Time involved: Five minutes

Supplies: Paper, pencils.

Purpose: To make the students think about a subject that will be taught.

How-to for CONTINUOUS SENTENCES:
Explain the procedure. Students are to make up a sentence about the Lord. Each word must begin with the letter the previous word ended with. An example for the study of Jesus' temptation might be:

JESUSAWEIRDEVILOOKINGHOSTLYELLOWITHORRIBLEVIL

Or if the lesson is on the life of Joseph, a sample sentence might be:

JOSEPHADREAMAKINGRIEFOREAL

The students can come up with original sentences. Allow time to share sentences with the class.

SS895

HAS DONE GOOD WORK IN THE **OLD TESTAMENT**

HAS DONE GOOD WORK IN THE **NEW TESTAMENT**

Congratulations

NAME _____

FOR DOING A GREAT JOB AT:

_____

_____

TEACHER _____

PASTOR _____

SS895